CARB-CYCLING-HEALTHY-EATING-WEIGHT LOSS-GUIDE

ANURADHA SRIVASTAVA

Contents

Prologue

Introduction

For anyone trying to lose weight, the word "carbs" is akin to blasphemy. Carb is the age-old enemy. Carbs are the evil nemesis of WeightWatchers everywhere. Carbs mean calories and weight loss requires cutting calories.

It has been the traditional belief that foods packed with carbs will cause you to pack on the pounds. Even healthy carbs like starchy vegetables and whole grains are high in carbs, so many classic diets restrict them as well. The result is that we have become to believe that carbs are bad for us. Not only do they hinder weight loss, but they are downright unhealthy.

Well, science has recently turned that belief upside down by telling us that carbs may be your best ally in the battle to lose weight. Leveraging carbs to help us lose weight is called carb cycling. it is a method whereby eating carbs can lead to weight loss rather than weight gain!

Carb cycling is done through a weekly eating plan with a few basic rules to stick to. Other than that, you have a full run of what you eat. Your meal plans can consist of all your favorite healthy foods, including carbs. You even have cheat days to indulge in your less healthy favorite foods to satisfy your cravings!

Why Is The 7-Day Plan Different?

Many of us struggle with our weight and strive to be fit and healthy. We've all experimented with different diets and eating regimens. We've tried diets that promised amazing weight loss, in X number of days. We've tried diets that promised we'd never feel hungry or sluggish. We've tried diets that you could eat everything and lose weight – only to find that "everything" meant in half spoonfuls.

We have been let down repeatedly. We either fall off the wagon and binge like crazy or get too discouraged to continue. Most, if not all traditional diets simply do not work for us.

What makes the carb cycling plan different? First, it makes a lot of sense because it addresses our metabolism ratherthan our stomach. After all, it's our metabolism that burns calories and melts off those pounds.

Secondly, although it has been recently hailed as a breakthrough in the field of healthy eating and weight loss, it has been popular among athletes for decades, especially those doing high resistance training. Many of them rely on carb cycling to build lean muscle and boost their energy levels.

Thirdly, a carb recycling plan is not as restrictive as other diets. It's therefore easy to follow.

Fourthly, the plan is used only to achieve shorter-term weight-loss goals, after which you must stop. However, you can use elements of it to develop lifelong healthy eating habits to stay fit and healthy for the rest of your life.

This is a very simple guide for the layman who wants to try the 7-day carb cycling plan. We will not go into the deeper technicalities of how carb recycling works, the different hormones it triggers nor discuss complex measurements. It will explain how and why carb cycling works, and what you need to do to put together your 7-day carb cycling plan. The results will speak for themselves.

So, if you are considering giving the carb cycling plan a try, this book will help you get started.

Here, I must insert the traditional disclaimer. If you suffer from any chronic illness or are taking any sort of medication, do consult your doctor before embarking on this plan.

Chapter 1 - How Carb Cycling Works

Remember how those old railway trains used to run? Workers had to stand in front of a huge coal furnace, shoveling in huge quantities of coal. If the furnace was regularly fueled, the train would keep running at full speed. If the coal input slowed down, the train would lose speed. If the furnace was not regularly fed with coal, the train would come to a standstill.

Our body's metabolism is very similar to this process. Carbs are the main food group that "fuels" our metabolism so that it burns calories and gives us energy. Carbs are also very filling. Therefore, diets that cut out or strictly limit carb intake make us feel tired and sluggish. They also make us irritable, hungry and more likely to binge.

With the 7-day carb cycling plan, a person consumes carbs to boost metabolism. The plan causes the body to use crab- rich foods to function at the optimal peak, burning fat and building muscle. The result is weight loss with less flab. It's that simple! This is what makes carb cycling unique and revolutionary.

But there's a catch. This doesn't mean going overboard with the carbs and eat tons of them day in, day out. The catch is that you follow a 7-day plan where you eat more carbs on certain days and less or no carbs on other days.

This allows your body to optimally "cycle" your carb intake so that you lose weight and build muscle mass.

The theory behind this is that on the days when your carb intake is low and fat intake is higher, your body is forced to burn fat for energy. This is what causes weight loss. The purpose of the High carb days is to keep your metabolism fueled and functioning peak level, providing you with energy.

What Is The 7-day Plan?

The weekly plan alternates high carb days with low carb days to keep your metabolism in a regular cycle of fat burning.

On high carb days, you can increase your carb intake while decreasing your fat intake. On low carb days, you can choose to eat small quantities of carbs or eliminate them altogether, while increasing fat and protein intake.

Athletes and people who exercise regularly often choose to synchronize their high carb days with practice or workouts when their energy levels are high. You may want to consider this for certain days when you are particularly active.

A typical 7-day plan looks like this:

Monday: High carb intake Tuesday: Low carb intake Wednesday: High carb intake. Thursday: Low carb intake.

Friday: High carb intake.

Saturday: High carb day – or the option of rewarding yourself. You can indulge (moderately) in your favorite foods. This is also called "cheat day". Sunday: Low carb day.

Versions of the 7-day plan

There are several versions of the plan where two or more high carb days will be followed by low carb days or some variation of this. Some examples are:

Alternative plan 1:

Day 1: High carbs Day 2: Low carbs Day 3: Zero carbs Day 4: Low carbs Day 5: High carbs Day 6: Low carbs Day 7: Zero carbs

Alternative plan 2:

Day 1: High carbs Day 2: Low carbs Day 3: Zero carbs Day 4: Low carbs Day 5: High carbs Day 6: Low carbs

Day 7: Zero carbs

There are a variety of other versions as well, such as 4 high carb days followed by three low carb days. However, as a beginner, you will want to start with the simple alternate day plan.

You can switch to a different cycle when you get the hang of it and feel you are ready. Or, you can stick to the basic plan throughout your journey until you have achieved your weight loss goal.

If you find that carb cycling works for you, you may want to delve deeper into these other plans. In this case, you will want to consult an expert. They will help you customize a plan that suits your weight goals, gender, and lifestyle.

The alternate-day plan we will use here is just the simplest for a beginner and will work for anyone.

What You Eat

Carbs: They are the main source of fuel for the body and essential for boosting metabolism. They are also essential for potting the fat-burning cycle into action.

Protein: This is the foundation of your carb cycling plan. You must eat between $1/5^{th}$ to $1/7^{th}$ of the minimum required daily intake with each meal.

Fats: Fat intake will remain consistent throughout the plan. You may raise your fat intake a little bit on low carb days for more energy.

Calculating your daily intake

For the best results, you need to calculate your daily intake of carbs, proteins, and fats. This a very easy process of multiplication

Low carb days

Carbs: Women simply must multiply their body weight by

0.6. Men should multiply bodyweight by 0.9. The resulting number will represent the carbohydrate intake in grams per day.

Proteins: Women can calculate their daily intake by multiplying their body weight by 1.2. Men can calculate their daily intake by multiplying their body weight by 1.5. The resulting number will be the required daily intake of protein per day.

Fats: To calculate daily fat intake, women should multiply their body weight by 0.5, while men should multiply by 0.8. The resulting number is your daily intake of fats in grams.

To calculate the total number of calories, add the totals from the three food groups.

High carb days

The same calculation is used, except that in this case, your intake of carbs and proteins will be higher. Your intake of fats will decrease.

Carbs: Women should multiply their body weight by 1.4 while men will multiply by 1.7.

Proteins: Women multiply their body weight by 1.4 and men by 1.7 (yes, it's the same ratio as for carbs)

Fats: Women should multiple bodyweight by 0.3 whereas men should multiply by 0.6.

The total of the three numbers will give you the total number of calories you can consume for High carb days.

It is up to you how you divide your daily intake throughout meals, whether you are having three meals or six meals per day.

Calories

As for daily calorie consumption, the recommended range is 1500 – 2300 for women and 1500 – 3000 for men. This is the general recommended range that you should stay within. However, don't beat yourself up if you exceed it a little on some days. I highly recommend that you invest in a calorie counting app. As for how many calories are contained in the foods you consume, you can easily look this up online and prepare a reference list to store on your computer.

Portions

Carb portions range from 200 grams to 300 grams on high carb days and 50 grams to 150 grams on lower carb days. We will discuss portions and food types in a later chapter.

This was a very simple explanation of how the carb cycling plan works. Next, let's find out why it works and how it can benefit you.

Chapter 2 - Why the Carb Cycling Diet Works

The carb cycling diet has become mainstream recently. Research is still ongoing with regards to the additional benefits. However, many people have reported great success with the 7-day plan for several reasons. Here are some of the arguments for why it works:

- One of the main reasons is flexibility. It really doesn't feel like a diet because there is a wide variety of foods to choose from. You can eat your favorite foods on certain days. People who follow the plan report not feeling deprived. And, the cheat day really helps as well!

- It gives you the ability to customize your plan if you stick to the basic rules.

- It can easily be adopted into your lifestyle and become permanent or a long-term eating habit.

- It is a simple protocol. Any layman who wants to lose

weight will have no trouble following the easy guidelines.

- Perhaps the strongest point is that it is proven simultaneously build muscle while burning fat. This is a dream come true for anyone who wants to shed stubborn pounds.

- A high carb diet has been shown to increase insulin production in the pancreas. This important hormone helps boost metabolism and energy levels. Insulin also helps maintain better body composition.

- The high carb intake increases the production of leptin, a hormone that decreases hunger.

- The high carb days will replenish and fuel glycogen, a compound that builds muscle

- You do not need to use elaborate measurements or track macronutrients. You will be able to see results by just monitoring daily calorie intake sticking to the basic guidelines.

Traditionally, it was believed that you could not build muscle and lose fat at the same time. This is because losing fat requires less calorie intake while building muscles requires more. Amazingly, carb cycling is the magic formula that helps the body do both. This is the real game-changer.

Carb cycling works because it's a healthy way to lose weight and get into better shape.

Chapter 3 - Starting off on the Right Foot

A little bit of preparation before starting your plan will save you a lot of time, hassle, and mistakes. Here are the basics you need to have in place to start off on the right foot.

Choose Your Plan

First, decide on which days will be your high carb days and which will be low carb days. For the purpose of simplicity, we will use the alternating high carb/low carb day plan. If you would like to use another of the versions described above, just switch the meal plans around to fit your days.

Ideally, your high carb days should correspond to days when you are the most active, However, this is not a rule. Next, pick your "cheat day".

This is the plan you will stick to for the next month. It is not recommended to switch plans midway as it will disrupt the existing cycle.

Decide On the Number of Meals

How many meals you eat per day is totally up to you. Some people prefer four to six smaller meals instead of the traditional three. This type of plan may suit you if you are used to snacking more during the day. The 3-meal plans include healthy snacks as well. If you are the type of person who frequently feels hungry, then more meals a day will work better.

More advanced carb cyclers may incorporate fasting or eating just two meals a day. However, this is not recommended for beginners.

Set Your Week's Meal Plan

This is the fun part! It's better to plan your meals weekly, biweekly or even monthly if you're really organized. This will save you the hassle of scrambling to put a meal together at the last minute.

The meal plan should list the day, whether it is a high or low carb day and the number of meals.

Each meal should be followed by the time you will have it. The times are just a general framework. You can have your next meal a little earlier on days when you feel hungry.

There are also be those crazy days when you just can't stick to your schedule. You can have meals a little later but don't skip them altogether so as not to disrupt your metabolism.

Include the portions of food you will have for each meal

Stock Up On The Food You Need

Your cupboards and fridge should have all the ingredients you need for your meal plans. It's a good idea to shop weekly for all the food that you need. You can freeze some foods; store others and vegetables will not have time to go bad. You will have some sample meal plans to guide you in a later chapter.

Remember that you must follow your chosen plan for at least four weeks before changing high carb and low carb days.

Stock Up On Long-Life Healthy Carbs

A lot of healthy carbs like potatoes, nuts, and legumes have a long shelf life. Buy them in bulk so that you never run out of carbs.

Recommended Food Portions

In addition to calorie and gram intake, the recommended quantities for carbs, some meal plans include portions in half-cups or cups (if you are using meal plans you found online for example). This is perfectly fine. There is no need for complicated conversions.

Notice that on low carb days, your fat and protein intake will be higher. Make sure you are eating healthy fats and proteins.

Invest in a small food scale easily measure gram and oz. portions.

To follow is the recommended daily intake of carbs, proteins, and fats.

HIGH CARB DAYS

FOOD TYPE
GRAMS PER
POUND OF BODY WEIGHT
Carbs
2 – 2.5 gm.
Proteins
1 gm.
Fats
0 -0.15 gm.-

LOW CARB DAYS
FOOD TYPE
GRAMS PER BODY WEIGHT
Carbs
0.5 gm.
Proteins
1.5 gm
Fats
0.35

Once you have these basics set up, you are now ready for the next step – what to eat and what to avoid.

Chapter 4 - What to Eat and What to Avoid

Healthy vs. Unhealthy Carbs

First and foremost, you need to eat healthy carbs and avoid unhealthy carbs like the plague. Healthy carbs are known as complex or unprocessed carbs. Processed carbs are those that are loaded with useless calories and really have zero nutritional value.

This is one restriction that you really need to follow for your carb plan to work. So, if you are addicted to white bread, summon up the willpower to avoid it except for maybe one slice on cheat days. Luckily, the list of healthy carbs is so varied that there is something on it for everyone.

HEALTHY UNPROCESSED
CARBS
UNHEALTHY COMPLEX CARBS
Brown rice
White or whole wheat

flour
Natural sweeteners like
honey or molasses
Table sugar
Whole grain bread
Processed cereals
Whole grain pasta
Store-bought cookies
and cakes
Sprouted grains like buckwheat, oats, and
quinoa
Soft drinks
White potatoes
Pizza
Sweet potatoes
French fries
Lentils
white pasta
All types of beans and
legumes
Muffins
Butternut squash
Tortillas and wraps
Oatmeal
Processed chips and
similar snacks
Corn
Ice cream
Peas
Jams and jellies
Couscous
Processed fruit juices

Fruits rich in carbs like bananas, peaches, plums, pineapple, and

blueberries

Bagels and pretzels

Beets

Chocolate and candy

Some vegetable with low amounts of carbs include tomatoes, mushrooms, cabbage, Brussel sprouts, and

peppers.

Pancakes

Dates

Beer

Healthy vs. Unhealthy Fats And Proteins Vegetables, proteins, and fats are the basis of your low carb days. But if you're eating unhealthy fats and proteins on low carb days, that just defeats the purpose. Healthy fats and proteins not only boost the process of carb cycling but also give you more energy. Make sure you include a good variety of these in your plan.

HEALTHY DAYS AND PROTEINS FOR LOW CARB DAYS

UNHEALTHY FATS AND PROTEINS

Grass-fed lean meat

Processed meats like

bacon, pastrami and

luncheon meats

Organic eggs

Hot dogs and sausage

Poultry

Fish, especially that

high in healthy Omega-3 fats like tuna, salmon, and

mackerel

Heavy cream and milk

Raw dairy products
like goat cheese, feta, and ricotta
Peanut butter
Low-fat dairy
products
Nuts and seeds
Olive oil, palm oil
Leafy greens and all non-starchy
vegetables
Avocadoes
Apples and apricots
Almond butter

Hopefully, you get the idea. Now, you can begin to incorporate healthy foods into your meals and start carb cycling!

Chapter 5 - Sample Meal Plans

Putting all this information into a concrete meal plan can be daunting for beginners. These sample meal plans for a typical carb cycling week should help. Use them as a basic blueprint for designing your meals but remember, it's not carved in stone. You can add or discard meals according to your chosen 7-day plan.

PLAN 1

Monday (low carb day)

Breakfast

- 3 whole eggs, scrambled, poached boiled or fried.
- 1/2 cup of high-carb fruit like blueberries, pineapple or peaches
- 1/cup oatmeal sweetened with honey

Snack

- I apple or 1/2 cup unsalted nuts

Lunch

- Turkey sandwich with lettuce and tomato on whole-wheat bread.
- Herbal tea

Snack

- 1/2 cup ricotta cheese or 2 medium apricots

Dinner

- Spinach Frittata
- Grilled beef strips with green bell peppers
- Green salad

Tuesday (High carb day)

Breakfast

- Two slices whole wheat bread with Swiss cheese
- 1 cup low-fat yogurt with fresh blueberries

Snack

- 1 banana

Lunch

- Grilled salmon with brown rice
- Grated carrot and cucumber salad

Snack

- 1 slice whole wheat bread with almond butter

Dinner

- Whole wheat pasta with fresh tomatoes
- Black beans with garlic oil
- Fresh green salad

Wednesday (low carb day)

Breakfast

- 3 scrambled eggs with avocado

Snack

- 2 apricots or 2 plums

Lunch

- Caesar salad with grilled chicken strips
- Herbal tea

Snack

- Low-fat yogurt or 1/2 cup of nuts

Dinner

- Flank steak with green beans and onions
- Green salad with feta cheese

Thursday (High carb day)

Breakfast

- 2 poached eggs
- 2 slices whole-wheat toast
- 1/2 cup fruit

Snack

- 1/2 cup fruit or nuts or 1 banana

Lunch

- 1 cup brown rice with chickpeas
- Sweet potatoes
- Green salad

Snack

- Low-fat yogurt with honey or 1 banana

Dinner

- Baked potato
- Grilled chicken breast
- Avocado and tomato salad

Friday (low carb day)

Breakfast

- 1/2 cup oatmeal
- 1/2 cup fruit
- 1/2 cup ricotta, feta or goat cheese

Snack

- 1/2 cup fruit or nuts or 1 low-fat yogurt

Lunch

- Avocado and chicken salad
- Sliced tomatoes on lettuce
- Herbal tea

Snack

- 1 orange or 1 apple or 2 plums

Dinner

- Grilled salmon with vegetables
- Naked beans
- Green salad

Saturday (high carb day)

Breakfast

- 2 scrambled eggs on whole-wheat toast
- 1 low-fat yogurt sweetened with honey

Lunch

- Sweet potatoes

- Lentil soup

Snack

- 1/2 cup nuts or fruit

Dinner

- Tuna Casserole Whole wheat noodles
- Spinach salad

Sunday (low carb + cheat day)

Breakfast

- Lean sausages with fried eggs
- 1/2 cup fruit

Snack

- Almond butter or 1/2 cup nuts

Lunch

- Tuna salad
- 1 piece of fresh fruit

Snack

- 2 plums, two apricots or 1 apple

Dinner:

Whatever you want! In moderation, please. For example, have two slices of pizza instead of two or three. Indulge in a moderate portion of ice cream or cake. If you've been craving French fries all week, eat a small plate of them, not a whole platter. You get the idea.

PLAN 2

If you prefer more than three meals a day, here is a sample plan to guide you.

TYPICAL LOW CARB DAY

Meal 1

- 3 egg
- 3 strips of lean bacon
- Sautéed peppers

Meal 2

- 4 oz. grilled turkey or chicken breast
- 1 cup carrots
- Lettuce and tomato salad

Meal 3

- 4 0z grilles salmon, tuna or shrimp
- 1 cup broccoli
- 1 banana

Meal 4

- 4 oz. chicken
- 1 cup spinach
- 1 low-fat yogurt with honey

Meal 5

- 4 oz. tuna
- 1 cup chickpeas
- 1 sliced tomato or cucumber

Meal 6

- 4 oz. lean steak
- 1 cup green beans
- 1/2 cup fruit

TYPICAL HIGH CARB DAY

Meal 1

- 2 eggs
- 3 strips of bacon or 3 small sausages
- 2 slices whole-wheat toast

Meal 2

- 4 oz. chicken
- Green salad
- 1/2 cup oatmeal sweetened with honey

Meal 3

- 4 oz. salmon
- 1/2 cup brown rice
- 1/2 cup carrots and peas

Meal 4

- 4 oz. chicken
- 2 cups spinach
- 1 cup arb-rich fruit like peaches, plums or apricots

Meal 5

- 1 cup of corn
- 1 sliced cucumber
- 1/2 cup of wild rice or quinoa

Meal 6

- 4 oz. grilled beefsteak
- 1 yam
- 1 cup green beans
- Green salad

PLAN 3

Here is a third meal plan sample that just includes several suggestions for each day, letting you calculate the portions as you learned in a previous chapter.

Low carb day

Breakfast

- Egg muffins
- Sour cream with chives
- 1 banana

OR...

- Whole wheat pancakes with cream cheese
- 3 sausages
- Blueberries or diced pineapple

Lunch

- Tacos with lean ground beef
- Green salad
- 1 piece whole fruit

OR...

- Bell peppers stuffed with lean ground beef
- Sliced cucumber and spinach topped with grated parmesan cheese
- 1 apple

OR...

- Chicken salad on lettuce
- Baked butternut squash with herbs
- Fruit salad

Dinner

- Whole wheat pasta with grilled chicken strips and parmesan cheese
- Green beans with carrots

OR...

- Beef stroganoff with mushrooms
- Brown rice
- Shredded lettuce and tomato salad
- Jelly cup

OR...

- Chicken fajita wraps
- Zucchini boats stuffed with mozzarella
- Green salad
- 1 piece whole fruit

Snacks

- Rice cake with almond butter
- Protein shake
- Hummus dip and celery sticks
- Strawberry and banana smoothie
- Cottage cheese with honey

- Cream cheese with herbs and carrot sticks

HIGH CARB DAYS

Breakfast

- Scrambled eggs with bacon and chives
- Oatmeal with blueberries and honey
- 1 piece whole fruit

OR...

- Boiled eggs
- 2 slices whole-wheat bread with cream cheese
- 1 banana

OR...

- Fried eggs with sausage
- 2 slices whole what toast
- 1 yam

Lunch

- Grilled turkey sandwich
- Chickpea salad
- Yogurt with honey

OR...

- Grilled salmon
- Sweet potato and spinach salad
- 1 piece whole fruit

OR...

- Shrimp with whole wheat noodles
- Potato salad
- 1 piece whole fruit

Dinner:

- Baked chicken
- Mexican brown rice
- Peas with carrots
- 1 piece whole fruit

OR...

- Pan steak with potatoes
- Broccoli with sweet corm
- Jelly cup

OR...

- Pasta with chicken and mushroom
- Cherry tomato and spinach salad
- Quinoa sweetened with honey

As you can see, there is huge room to get creative and once up with mouthwatering, meals. Once you get the hang of it, you will be able to come up with delicious treats for the whole family to enjoy along with you (although family members not on the plan or kids should not restrict themselves to portions or calories.

You can also tweak your favorite recipes to make them carb cycling-friendly by replacing processed carbs with healthy ones, and saturated fats with good fats.

Chapter 6 - Normal Side Effects to Expect

Don't worry. The side effects are nothing remotely dangerous. Consider them as minor symptoms that may cause some discomfort.

Any disruptive changes in diet or exercise routines may have some temporary side effects. It's like when you work out after a period of inactivity. Your muscles will ache for a couple of days afterward. But you know it's a result of your workout.

Some people starting the carb cycling plan have reported experiencing some side effects. These should pass or decrease significantly within a week or so.

1. Water weight gain. Expect to see some water weight gain especially on high carb days. This is because your body stores four times more water for every gram of carbs you consume. This should normalize over time.

You will notice less water weight gain on low carb days. So, rest assured that you are not gaining real weight.

Exercising on high carb days may also help with this issue. Note: Despite this water weight gain, you still need to drink lots of water throughout the day.

1. You may feel more tired and lethargic than usual during the first week or so. This is normal. You will regain your usual energy – in fact, you will notice increased energy - once the carb cycling kicks in.

3. You may experience constipation or bloating. This is due to your high carb intake, especially more starchy foods like potatoes and rice.

Herbal teas, especially chamomile, is a wonderful cure for this. You can also replace your fruit intake with stewed fruit until your digestion improves.

4. You may feel irritable and experience mood swings. This is a normal complaint.IT could be that for you, the carb cycling plan is restrictive What does that mean? If you are used to eating more carbs than the quantities prescribed in this plan, then you are restricting yourself. This deprivation may cause some irritability and moodiness for the first few days.

5. You may experience cravings due to the switch from unhealthy carbs and fats to healthy ones. Willpower and the cheat day will help you overcome this.

6. Your body may crave more carbs on low carb days.

Other than the above, the harmless side effects, there is no real danger in following a carb cycling diet. However, always listen to what your body tells you. If these side effects last for more than two weeks, then the carb diet may just not for you.

Custom Keto Diet Top Product

Chapter 7 – Helpful Tips

Here are some sensible tips to make your carb cycling plan more effective. You may be practicing some of them already.

1. Cheat days are not an open invitation to go overboard and stuff yourself with all your favorite food. Have a slice of pizza or a Big Mac if you're really craving that. Just remember that the cheat day is there as an option and not as a mandate.

Your carb cycling results depend on how much you "cheat". If you do it every week then, of course, your weight loss will be slower. If you want faster results, keep cheat days to a minimum.

2. Don't skip breakfast and always make sure you eat protein and fiber. This is essential for beating those cravings and keeping you full until the next meal

3. Consider resistance or aerobic exercise to maintain your muscle mass and make the most of carb cycling. If this doesn't appeal to you, any exercise you prefer will be beneficial. Walking, cycling or swimming are good

alternatives.

4. If you are active in sports or work out regularly, synchronize high carb days with your high activity days. This will help you shed those pounds faster. Plus, you will have higher energy levels on those days.

5. Avoid "drinking" your calories. This includes smoothies, sweetened tea, and coffee or fruit juices. Stick to water or herbal tea. If you must have your morning coffee, try to take it black. As for tea, it doesn't taste too bad when sweetened with honey.

6. Supplements can maintain your carb cycling at an optimal level and improve digestions. Omega-3, Vitamin B 12 and probiotics are good choices.

7. Get creative with meal plans. Work with the wide variety of foods that you have, to create delicious dishes. Search online for new recipes to try and experiment with new carb combinations. Also, experiment with things you've

never tried before, like quinoa, kale or hummus. You might be pleasantly surprised!

8. Get enough sleep to stay energetic and avoid stress. Give your body the rest it needs for optimal carb cycling. This is just good common sense for anyone striving for better health.

Conclusion

This was a simple presentation of the carb diet and how it works. We have covered all the information you need to know to get started.

So, what are the main takeaways?

- Carb cycling works by fueling your metabolism to burn fat and build muscle simultaneously.

- Carb cycling is based on a 7-day plan where you have high carb days and low carb days.

- You plan your meals around the recommended daily intake of carbs, proteins, and fats for that day.

- You lose weight!

Diets that eliminate carbs just don't work for everybody.

The deprivation and resulting cravings can be too much.

Because the 7-day carb cycling plan is not restrictive, you have a much higher chance of sticking to it. Even on low carb days, you are still able to eat carbs. This could possibly be the easiest and least painful way of losing weight.

If you find the flexibility and wide variety of foods appealing, then it's worth a try. It is certainly far less rigid and restricting, and people have reported that they hardly ever feel hungry. And of course, there is the ultimate benefit of losing weight and building muscle mass simultaneously. So, go ahead, stock up on healthy carbs and proteins, have fun with your meal plans, and start looking better, feeling better and getting in shape today.

https://sites.google.com/view/health-supplements09/home

Printed by Libri Plureos GmbH in Hamburg,
Germany